Sandy Dann's
Oldlando

The Legacies of the Dann and Lawson Families as Early Settlers of Orlando and Central Florida

The Lawson family owned Stone Island on the St. John's River facing Sanford. The swampy cypress filled terrain was one of the family-owned playgrounds for adventurous young Sandy Dann.

COPYRIGHT

Title:
Sandy Dann's Oldlando
The Legacies of the Dann and Lawson Families
as Early Settlers of Orlando and Central Florida

as Recalled by Dr. Carl "Sandy" Dann, III

Published by:
Cutting Edge Communications, Inc.
P.O. Box 476, Winter Park, FL 32790 USA

2014 and 2015 Interviews of Sandy Dann by:
Casey Tennyson Swann

International Standard Book Number
ISBN number 978-0-692-40257-3

Other books about Dr. Carl "Sandy" Dann, III:

Sandy and Shelia Dann were honored in a book commissioned in
2012 by their partners in an estancia as a surprise gift to them titled
*The Hunt For Nirvana, The Gentlemen Ranchers of El Saladero, Uruguay,
A Collection of Stories and Images from 2004 to 2011.*

and
*Dreadful Errors in Judgement
The Wild Worldwide Stories of Native Florida Outdoorsman
Carl "Sandy" Dann, III*
about Sandy hunting, fishing and exploring all over the world where
he nearly died many times but lived to tell the tales.

INTRODUCTION

THE GIST: This is a book about Orlando, which is what all of Central Florida was called in the pioneer and early days. My mother's and father's families were opposite types of Floridians. My grandfather Dann had no education and was a self made man. My grandfather Lawson was educted and eurodite. The conflicts of these two families mirrored the conflicts of the early population at large as they all communally created the blueprints for what is now a major city. My last book was about myself and my adventures hunting and fishing. This book is about many things that happened before my time. The stories passed down to me, now I am passing on. Based in Orlando, my own story has been memorable and pleasurable. I wouldn't live anywhere else, and I've been everywhere. Orlando is my home.

Sandy Dann boated and fished summers back in Orlando, from prep school, with friends such as George Delay, Bob Crieg, Tom Sawyer, Stu Gilman and Sandy Dann heading the boat.

CONTENTS

CHAPTERS

Sandy's outdoor hunting and fishing adventures growing up in Orlando fueled a lifelong love of the outdoors and exotic animal explorations worldwide. A sketch by Sandy in his childhood photo album showed his early interest in nature. His education took him from Orlando for 30 years. His exotic explorations lured him all over the world throughout his life. Orlando would always beckon him home.

Sandy's grandfather Carl Dann, Sr. wrote the humorous *Vicissitudes and Casathropics* in 1939 and his more serious grandfather William Claiborne Lawson wrote *The Quest for Self-Government* in 1941. Sandy was influenced greatly by both grandfathers.

I was born Carl "Sandy" Dann, III in 1932 in Orlando, Florida. All of Central Florida was often called "Orlando" then.

My story pivots around a conflict in the way of life of two Old-Florida families, highlighted by the two grandfathers and how they influenced me. Both grandfathers were successful but had two different ways of life. On one hand, Florida Cracker grandfather Dann had a first and fourth grade education, and developed more than any other developer in Orlando since. He died when I was in second grade.

1924 Developer Carl Dann, Sr. at his home on Hillcrest St. He was born in 1885 and opened Dubsdread Country Club and golf course in 1924. The club is now owned by City of Orlando and open to the public.

At left, in 1936 Carl "Sandy" Dann, III, Carl Dann, Jr. and Carl Dann, Sr. at Dubsdread golf course hitting balls. Sandy's grandfather Dann built the second course in Orlando, Dubsdread. Orlando Country Club was the first. Dann would also build the third in Mt. Plymouth.

1

Sandy's grandfather Carl Dann,
Sr. was a significant developer in
Central Florida.
At right, Sandy's parents with his
sister Joanie at her wedding.

Sandy grew up in Orlando under the influence of his two grandfathers. He was a wrestler and an avid outdoorsman.

On the other hand, grandfather Lawson was the youngest person to pass the Bar in Washington, D.C. at that time, and brought his erudite sophistication from Washington to Central Florida with developments in downtown Orlando and Stone Island in Sanford. He ran for senate on the Republican ticket, thus, making Florida a two-party system. Until then, only Democrats ran in Florida so voters had only one choice. Both had a marked influence on the City Beautiful, and on my life.

My mother and father had different concepts of what life is about because they were raised totally opposite. I led my own life with the wit and wisdom from each family.

I grew up in Florida when it was barren. We built canoes and made tree houses. We did so many little fun things just being kids. I loved my childhood in Florida. It was truly the best of times.

My own family evolved along with Orlando in general. These two opposite lifestyles of the crackers and the educated elite would meld into a major metropolitan city.

In my childhood, Florida was a nasty town. There was a lot of bloodshed. It was the last of the gun-slinging towns. We still had Native American Indians, too. Some of the biggest crooks came and made it a violent area. Not just the cowboys of the Wild-West carried guns.

My family on the Dann side, moved here in 1745 when there were less than 20 people in the area. Now over three-million call Orlando area home. It's hard to imagine.

More people came after the Civil War. Many people don't know that some of the worst battles of the Civil War were fought in North Florida. There were a high number of deaths in Mosquito County, which later was re-named Orange County.

Three main families brought big amounts of money here. Men from the Beardall, Huckoll and Milligan families were the early mayors. The first two mayors were killed. The police were killed. It was not a nice little place to live. It was a vicious horror place. People were given the land by the government but couldn't survive here in the wilderness. My grandfather Dann wrote about what happened when he was a kid and what his grandparents told him. I continue to pass down the stories to my own family and friends.

The Dann family early settlers did not have formal educations. Sandy's father graduated from Rollins College and Sandy became a doctor. His grandfather founded his success as a developer on ingenuity and intellect, values he passed on to his cherished grandson. Young Sandy is at his home with great grandmother, his grandfather and father.

All of Central Florida was called "Orlando" in the early days. Mosquito County was later named Orange County. It was the Wild West, the last of the gun-slinging towns in the U.S.

Grandmother Dann married my grandfather when she was 14-years-old. She was right off the train from Atlanta. Her name was Louise and we called her Weeze. We still have two plants here at the Greens Ave. home that she brought with her from Atlanta.

She didn't drink alcohol. One time she asked, "So, what is in those martinis?" So, I made her one and we sat out on the porch with two of the darkies and they told me all the tales of all of Orlando. Since the help worked in all the homes, they knew all the stories about all of the original families. Like all communities, large or small, there was a dark underbelly that was known of but rarely spoken of openly. Orlando was a rough town. The uneducated crackers had conflicts with the educated landowners, and they all had guns. The business owners all had enemies. They would burn down buildings, and shoot people, and rape people. It was a wild place here before my time.

Before the Civil War, where Orlando is now was then Mosquito County. There were 100 people between what is now Jacksonville and Miami. The U.S. land grant given to my family a few generations back was on Lake Apopka on a hill overlooking the Goard's Neck. It is now a checkerboard of developments. Lake Apopka is right off west Interstate Four. The middle of the state has soft rolling hills and an elevation of 400-feet, as opposed to the coastal areas at 25-feet above sea level. In the hills, the wind would blow away the mosquitos making it desirable to settle there. This crystal clear lake at the time, drew bass fishermen from all over the world. The biggest bass ever was caught there. The Goard's Neck is where the water spews up from the spring 65-feet down in Lake Apopka.

When I was young, I was at Lake Apopka with my friends. I wanted to be the first person to dive down to the spring holding my breath and carve my name on the wall. To dive that far down, you take big breaths and fill your body with oxygen for three or four minutes, then sit for three minutes without a breath. That is how you train your body for free diving. So, I dove down there and the entrance to the spring was pouring up bubbles and I saw carved in the wall, "Kilroy was here." That was a World War II thing. There

6

were lots of names on the wall. I wasn't the first.

I've lived in Orlando since 1932, and this book captures my memories of life and history in Orlando.

THE IMPORTANCE OF WINDOW SCREENS AND AIR CONDITIONING TO POPULATE ORLANDO

You think of Florida today, and you think of beaches. In my childhood, there were thick mosquitos on the coast in the marshes at that time. People couldn't tolerate to live on the coast till they opened the waterways and the marshes so the water could flow in and out. The mosquitos breed in stagnant water and the marshes gave plenty of breeding ground. Orlando was much the same.

Florida was one of the forgotten states before World War II. It didn't have a medical or dental school in the state, because no small window screens or air-conditioning, so good reasons. If you couldn't keep the mosquitos out, nobody wanted to live here. The mosquitos carried diseases. To have transportation and housing and the foundations of a community, people would have to want to be here. It's hard to picture that now, with Florida being one of the most desirable places to live.

At that time, a cracker house would have to have 100 to 150 feet around the house of sand, with no grass or trees. The reason is the mosquitos have to have something to hang on to. The first screens were big at first so the mosquitos and sand fleas just came through.

After small screens were invented but before air conditioning, the cracker houses would have huge screened porches built to the windward side, attached but outside of the home so the wind could blow from three directions. Not exactly romantic, but the whole family would sleep on the porches in warm weather. The homes were built up so the wind could blow under the houses and up through the fireplaces in summer, pulled by big fans in the attic.

Once air conditioning was invented, Florida boomed big time. Florida was finally tolerable.

CHAPTER 3, THE HOUSEHOLD

The first memory I have is when I was around five-years-old and we moved from downtown Orlando where I lived since birth in 1932, to a little house on Greens Ave. on Dubsdread Golf Course, which my grandfather Dann built. I live now in my paternal grandparent's home also on Greens Ave., on the sixteenth fairway. It was given to me by my grandmother Dann later in my life, when she passed. I live here today.

In my childhood, the houses were run by the black women help. We lived with two black ladies who had their own apartment with rooms and showers in the backside of the detached garage. Eddie Mae and Mabel were the maids, cooks and nannies. Sometimes a gardener lived with us. My father and mother were gone a lot, playing in golf tournaments and running the golf club.

Back then, we were punished severely by the blacks. They would make us pick our own switches off the trees. You learned that the smaller branches did not hurt less, maybe more. That's what they did back then in College Park.

I remember in the second and third grades going to school and people asking me, "What happened to you?" I would tell them that I had bugs bite me, or I fell out of a tree and got scratched, or I was crawling and lizards got me. Really the blacks gave spankings. I probably deserved it. You couldn't hide it because it was hot and we wore knee pants to school.

One time in second grade, my father was playing in a tournament. I got on the roof and peeled off the shingles from half of the roof. I slung them and threw them all over the yard. The first time, I peeled them all off the front and the second time all off the back. I did it because I didn't want to be left behind with the staff. I would pick on my younger sister Joanie, too, and I'd really get it then.

Sandy and sister Joanie at home in the 1930s in Orlando in the College Park neighborhood.

CHAPTER 4, THE DANN FAMILY MOVES TO FLORIDA IN 1842

All Danns in America are from the same family tree in Scotland, and immigrated to the States. As best as we can figure, they left the old country of their own free will and under no duress. Francis Dann has a wedding certificate recorded in Stanford, Conn. in 1685.

His descendant Elliot S. Dann had a land grant from the U.S. government in 1842 for 250 acres. He married Mary Ann Brewer Dann and had 13 children, the seventh being Hanford Dann in 1852. Hanford married Mary Graves and died in 1894 leaving her and four children. The third child was H. Carl Dann was born in 1885, my grandfather. They lived then at Long Street in Orlando.

In 1875, ten years before my grandfather was born, Orlando became an incorporated town of 85 people. Orlando was a tiny place.

Back to the first Danns settled in West Orlando on a hilltop in 1842. The big Lake Apopka on the property was crystal clear and filled with bass. They cut 150-feet every blade of grass and raked to just dirt around the house to take care of the mosquitos. The breeze also helped. The house was really a shack.

Every month-and-a-half a boat would come down the St. John's River to bring essentials to survive. There was a trail that led to the boat docking area. They had to make the trail, of course. It took two days to get there and two days back by horse. The landing in Sanford didn't exist then, so the boat would come from Jacksonville to the shallows on south of Sanford to leave the supplies. The government wanted the land settled, so they gave the family the land. They lived in that area for four generations. They were true Florida crackers and immigrated throughout Central Florida.

They then settled in what is now downtown Orlando with less than 100 other families at the time. Envision this beautiful place we now call Central Florida with all the flowing clear lakes. There is a giant spring on the first golf course, Orlando Country Club, with a natural 80-foot well, where the water boils out and drops down 17-feet to the next lake. That spring feeds the whole lake chain to the St. Johns River. The marshlands around the Orlando Country Club are where the Everglades begins.

My grandfather Dann wrote the whole story of how the lakes are all connected. The early people dug wells and filled in waterways to make navigable roads. The development changed the waterways and their flow patterns.

The Dann family was among the first twenty families in Central Florida. The subsequent generations prospered as the area grew in population and affluence.

Carl Dann, Jr.(father), Catherine Dann (mother), Joanie Dann (sister), Grandmother Louise, and Sandy Dann as a teenager

CHAPTER 5, GRANDFATHER CARL DANN, SR. ON SANDY'S FATHER'S SIDE

DEVELOPER CARL DANN, SR.

My grandfather Dann didn't believe in education, although my father, Carl Dann, Jr., went to Rollins College in Winter Park. My grandfather Dann succeeded without a formal education. He built 62 developments in Orange County. He built the second and third golf courses. He is the biggest developer to date in Central Florida. Nobody else even comes half way. If you stood at the corner of Orange and Central Avenues in downtown Orlando and turned around in a circle, every six degrees you would see one of his developments in the old days. In his newspaper ads, he promoted himself as "the man who was born without a dollar in his pocket ... in fact, he had no pocket." He was a self-made man.

Grandfather Dann had a first and fourth grade education. His dad died when he was in the first grade. He had to get a job, so he skipped second and third grade. He went back in forth grade and then quit for good. As a child, he had a goat route to help feed his two sisters and his mother. He had a cart and sold vegetables to people.

As I knew him when I was a child. He lived in downtown Orlando in a house that is still there on the corner of Hillcrest and Cathcart Streets. I lived in that house my first four years. I don't have much memory of that. My mother wanted her own house, so she convinced my father to move to Dubsdread, which had been built in 1926, in a little house at 510 W. Par Ave. I moved into my grandparents' home at 3206 Greens Ave. built in 1935 around 1960 when my grandmother fell ill and I inherited the house.

GRANDFATHER DANN WAS A MOTIVATIONAL SPEAKER

He was a developer and a humorous motivational speaker and gave lectures all over. He was a total character with Will Rogers-type humor. For example, he made a family crest which is in his book published in 1929, Vicissitudes and Casathrophics. The crest has a Florida jackass, a Florida boar, the signs he used for his real estate company, a Florida longhorn and a Latin saying that translates to, "No cow shit." He was hysterical.

The Dann family shield in Carl Dann, Sr.'s book *Vicissitudes and Casathrophics*. His humor endeared him to his family and friends.

FLORIDA CRACKERS

Grandfather Dann would pick me up at 10 a.m. He would take me out of school to hunker with the crackers. That's where you don't sit on the ground, but you hunker with crackers to hear stories about survival in wild Florida. I missed most of first grade and three months of second grade, because he didn't believe in school and would come pick me up and take me out to teach me about life. "I'll teach you what you need to know," he would tell me. The camp was along the lakes towards where Disney is now. The crackers would meet and drink booze that they made. They would climb up in the trees in the lake and dive off. I was so young. I didn't understand their language, and thick accents. I still have some cracker in me.

There was a big conflict about me missing school with my mother's side of the family. My mother would be screaming at my father about this. My father would be playing golf, and chasing women, and having a wonderful life.

Grandfather Dann died at 55-years-old when I was in second grade. He was born in 1885 and died in 1940. He died of a ruptured appendix. He didn't believe in doctors or medicine any more than he believed in formal education. So he died young. If he had lived, I might never have gone to school.

A Sam Stoltz original painting signed, "To Carl Dann the miser," is one of the historical artifacts in the Dann home. Sam Stoltz created elaborate detailing in his building with wood carvings, stained glass, wrought iron art, original paintings. Every house and building was uniquely created as an artful ediface.

GRANDFATHER DANN'S BUILDING STYLE WITH ARCHITECT / ARTIST SAM STOLTZ

Sam Stoltz was the artist and architect for my father's buildings including the family home on Greens Ave. off Par Ave., to the south across from Dubsdread Club.

Sam Stoltz lived in Winter Park. There are still a dozen of his homes in Winter Park, including mine. He built them to last. Each one is a work of art with exquisite artistic handcrafted detailing. Each one is unique. He came from New England. His wife was bedridden for 30 years during the time he befriended my grandfather.

Every Sam Stoltz house has birds on the outside. It might be in painted reliefs, frescoes, wrought iron detailing, or at our house, it's a stained glass feature. You can see the artistic detailing of the Sam Stoltz style in the wildlife images integrated in the hand hewn wrought iron banister on the steps going into the guest room, and into metal lamps and light fixtures.

Stained glass features and hand blown glass and etched fish in the tiles in the bathroom layer the artistic detailing. The artistic expression of Florida wildlife flows through the home.

The signature high ceilings of pecky cypress and several ornate stone fireplaces are throughout the house. The master bedroom fireplace has an intricately carved wood relief of wildlife.

The original two-bedroom house, still has the original kitchen. A separate bedroom was built on during World War II for officers to live who were stationed in Orlando. The porch leading to the guest room was enclosed to make a dining room. The garage is where the staff lived. A large library filled with books, and a family room complete the home, all still in perfectly maintained condition. Everybody in town helped house the service men who came to train for the Air Force.

A centerpiece in the guest room is a signed Sam Stoltz original painting signed, "To Carl Dann the miser." Sam Stoltz gave that to my grandfather when my grandfather refused to pay for work Sam did at the Mt. Plymouth golf course.

The Dann family home on Greens Ave. sits across from Dubsdread Golf Course in Orlando where Sandy grew up and still lives. Every detail of the home tells a tale as interesting as the man who lives there.

The architectural detailing is a Sam Stoltz design. Sandy's character is vibrantly added with collectibles from his worldwide travels.

Sandy's living room was filled with trophies before 42 went to a museum outside of Atlanta in Decateur. The Dann family home has the Sam Stoltz signature elements such as the stone fireplace, the pecky cypress ceilings, the handcrafted wrought iron detailing in the bannister, hand hewn light fixtures and other artistic details.

A vintage postcard of the Mt. Plymouth Hotel featuring developer Carl Dann, Sr. and artist / architect Sam Stoltz. The pair built Mt. Plymouth after they built Dubsdread together.

A vintage postcard of Dubsdread created by developer Carl Dann, Sr. and artist / architect Sam Stoltz. Sandy's mother and sister are two of the ladies seated on the lawn.

CHAPTER 6, GRANDFATHER DANN BUILT DUBSDREAD GOLF COURSE and CLUB

Dubsdread was the first of two golf courses grandfather Dann built. Dubsdread was the second golf course in Orlando and owned by my family for 60 years before we sold it to the city of Orlando. Orlando Country Club was the first. Originally, like many private clubs in the U.S., women and Jews could not be members at Orlando Country Club. During the depression, Orlando Country Club went bankrupt. The members came to grandfather Dann and asked him to loan money to restart the course. My grandfather agreed with the deal that Jewish people and women could play golf and make it not such a stuck-up place. Blacks then were caddies; they didn't play. It was another era. After the deal was sealed, the Orlando Country Club members changed their minds and changed the deal, which pissed off my grandfather. So, he looked for a piece of property in the marshland near the country club. He found a cattle farm with lakes all around and acquired it in 1924. Dubsdread Country Club would be built in the marsh with hills and greens just seven miles from the other course. He dug huge water holes and used soil to build the golf course and surrounding area. He built houses around all of the holes. He didn't make money on the golf course. He made money building and selling the houses on all the holes. In early 1900's Edgewater Drive was a dirt road. If you look at an aerial shot from Orange Avenue and Edgewater Drive where College Park now is, there were huge marshy lakes that were all connected. The developers, including my grandfather dug the lakes, built up land for development, and created a boom. The whole area boomed with wealthy people who came and bought land around the golf course. The price of a 25-foot lot was $25, 50-foot $50, and 100-foot $100.

The course stayed in the family, and my sister Joanie and my mother ran it. We each owned one-third. My sister had three kids at home, and my mother was exhausted. It was a 365 day-a-year endeavor. They wanted to sell the club. The City of Orlando wanted to buy the club for $2 million. A million was a lot of money then.

I was in Africa for a month when they reached an agreement with Mayor Carl Langford. They told me, "The city talked us down a little to $1 million." The city got 28 undeveloped lots along the golf course, the club and all the equipment. In my opinion that was more than 'a little', but the women wanted to get rid of the burden of running Dubsdread, so they agreed. In February 1978 the club became a public course.

We still dine there often. It's a block from the house on Greens Ave. Steve Gunter who runs the restaurant now does a great job. The food is excellent. It's the best restaurant in Orlando.

Today Dubsdread is a public golf course. The Taproom at Dubs-dread displays historic photos and postcards of Dubsdread's early years. According to Sandy Dann, the menu is better than ever and it's the "best restaurant in Orlando."

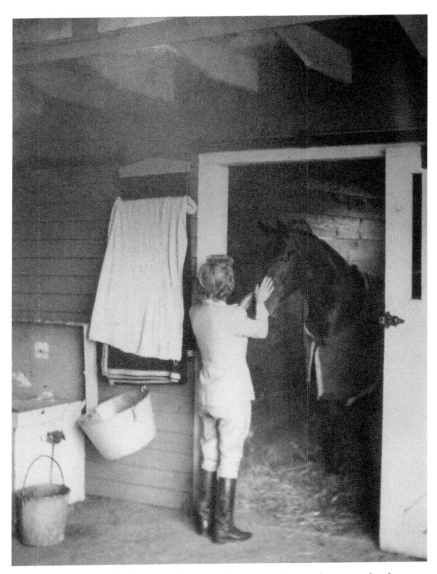

Sandy's mother Catherine Lawson Dann is shown here at the horse stables that were a part of Dubsdread Country Club. Catherine and Sandy's sister Joanie ran the club until they sold it to the City of Orlando in 1978.

CHAPTER 7, GRANDFATHER DANN BUILT MT. PLYMOUTH HOTEL, SPA AND GOLF COURSE FUNDED IN PART BY MOBSTER AL CAPONE

The third golf course in Orlando was built by grandfather Dann in Mt. Plymouth, between Apopka and Mt. Dora in Lake County. Mt. Plymouth was the neighborhood they developed in the town of Sorrento. It had it's own post office at one time.

The families there are big on local history and tradition. The East Lake Historical Society Museum at the corner of State Road 46 and County Road 437, has a room dedicated to the historic hotel. The Society also created Mt. Plymouth Memorial Park at the site of the hotel with the concrete entrance, which is all that remains. The hotel and development was a significant event for the ranchers and citrus families of that area. It was wilderness and basically still is. Wild turkeys still run around on the fairways. It's farmland.

The museum hotel room has renderings of the hotel and a photo of my grandfather Dann, sitting on a fence, smoking a cigar in front of his weekend log cabin a block from the hotel. The caption says, "You can take the Cracker out of the woods, but you cant' take the woods out of the Cracker."

Historic aerial view of the Mt. Plymouth Hotel built in 1927

Carl Dann's log cabin, where he stayed when visiting the Mt. Plymouth Hotel, still stands at 25343 Troon Ave. in Sorrento. The current owners won a 2011 Historical Home Award. The home is still a centerpiece of the community and hosts Santa Visits and such. Sandy visited the home in 2015.

The Mt. Plymouth pool in the 1930's wtih inset photo of one of the investors of the hotel complex, Al Capone.

The housing development was built around the Mt. Plymouth Hotel, Country Club and Spa. The hotel was built in 1926 and 1927 with my grandfather as developer and Sam Stoltz as the architect. It had a 150-room 4-story hotel with huge cathedral ceilings. It had wonderful stables for riding horses. It had polo, trap shooting, quail shooting, water sports and bass fishing.

There were five Sam Stoltz homes on the property. Several of them are still inhabited, some maintained better than others. One home, the log cabin style, was owned by my grandfather. Remember he died when I was in second grade so I don't remember visiting him at that house. He built the hotel six years before I was born.

Understand that not many people were here before World War II, so the wealthy people would come into airstrips on the property and taxi right up to the front entrance of the hotel. That was the plan.

In 1926, Al Capone put up money to build the course, along with 25 other people in Orlando, mostly wealthy politicians and landholders. It cost $350,000. Capone was the most notorious gambler

Photos such as this one of the airport adjoining the Mt. Plymouth Club and Hotel are archived at the East Lake Historical Society Museum in Sorrento, Fla.

that ever lived as the head of the Chicago mob. He was The Boss. I'm not sure how my grandfather contracted with Capone because I wasn't around. Capone would go to Miami, then stop in Orlando to play golf at Orlando Country Club and gamble at Dubsdread. So my grandfather knew him for some reason or another long before I was born. They were both big gamblers. Capone put up big money to build the course, and where he got the money is your guess.

There were four runways for airplanes to land and a tower from which Al Capone's bodyguards kept watch. In photos, you see four planes all lined up to head in different directions. There was a straight six-mile paved road to nowhere. It dead ended into the golf course and was the only entrance. Capone built a secret tunnel so he could escape if his boys saw police coming.

To understand the history of Florida, you have to understand that there is a ridge going down the middle of the state, with rolling hills. Since the course was on the uplands, it was not just flatland golf. The concept was for four golf courses with different types of fairways similar to world-class courses in Georgia and Ashville, North Carolina. Each of them would have a different design, which you could do in hill country with the variations in the terrain. They planned to attract people from all over the world to play on the courses.

27

The land was purchased inexpensively. The land was virtually valueless at the time. Today, if you go north past Apopka, to Plymouth Sorrento Road, it will take you past all the horse country and plant nurseries to the site of the hotel.

The first course was built called St. Andrews Course. This is not a fairway course. It was designed like the golf courses in Scotland. It had ponds all around the holes. Between tees, there would be woods or marshes. The course was in operation until 2012. Houses were constructed all around the course, just like the Dubsdread development concept.

My mother worked at the Mt. Plymouth club after high school, before she married my father. I played the course four or five times. My thing was hunting and hunting women and travel, not golf.

In 1929, the project collapsed because of the depression and the Stock Market crash, and the other golf courses on the property were never built. The investors parceled off the property and sold it.

Carl Dann, Sr. named the streets of his Mt. Plymouth Hotel, Dubsdread Dr. and Adair Dr. after his College Park / Orlando development.

Carl Dann, Sr.'s log cabin is a block from the entrance to the hotel. Mt. Plymouth Memorial Park is at the site of the hotel with the original entrance, a plaque and benches. Sandy Dann visited the memorial site in Jan. 2015. Historian Shirley Meade of the East Lake Historical Society said that it is her dream to erect a large 12-foot by 12-foot realistic mural of the hotel at the park.

The hotel turned into a boarding prep school, Florida Central Academy. From 1959 to 1983, for 24 years a lot of foreign students attended there. There were not a lot of fancy schools back then. A few of my friends today at the University Club went to that school. It was very high end. It was vacant from 1983 to 1986 for three years. Kids from Orlando said it was haunted and would have séances in the vacant hotel. In 1986 some kids got pissed and burned it down. All that is left is two white walls of the original entrance. All of that history and the Sam Stoltz artwork is gone.

As of 2015, the golf course land has been purchased by a developer and it's rumored that it will be developed with houses. It will be a shame that the original houses and the houses built up until this point now will not enjoy the scenic Florida views envisioned and created by my grandfather.

The Mt. Plymouth Hotel was vacant for three years after it had been a boarding school, then burned by teenagers in 1986.

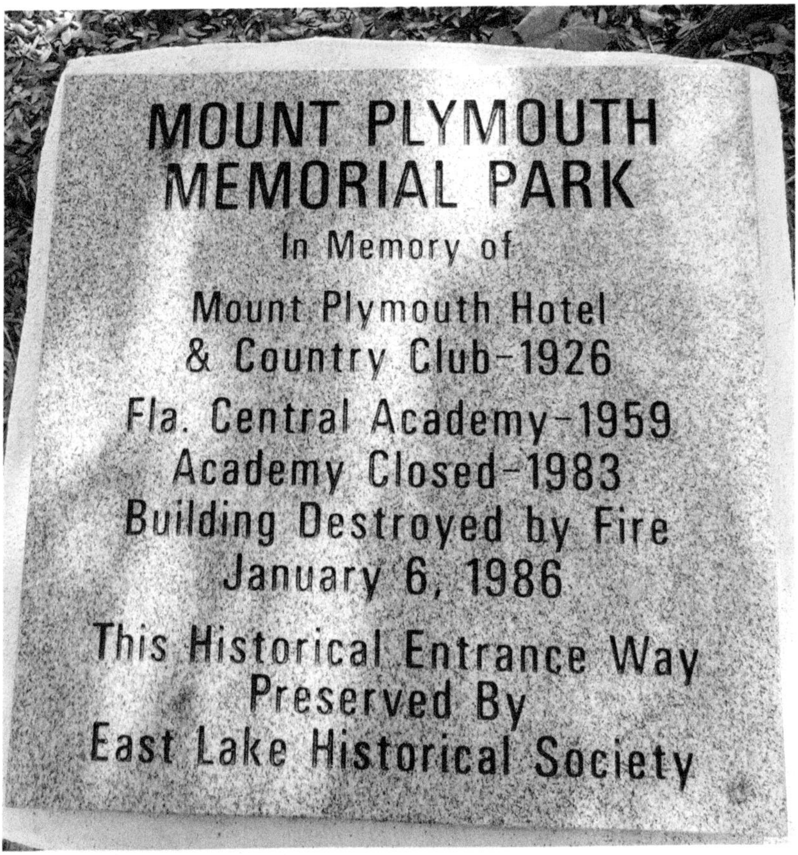

MOUNT PLYMOUTH
MEMORIAL PARK
In Memory of

Mount Plymouth Hotel
& Country Club-1926
Fla. Central Academy-1959
Academy Closed-1983
Building Destroyed by Fire
January 6, 1986

This Historical Entrance Way
Preserved By
East Lake Historical Society

We were very close.

Sandy with Grandmother Dann. She took him to see the premiere showing of the film *Gone With The Wind* in Atlanta. She would take him to Atlanta for summer vacations when he was young.

CHAPTER 8, GRANDMOTHER LOUISE "WEEZE" GILES DANN

ATLANTA TRIPS and GONE WITH THE WIND

When I was very young, my grandmother Dann, I called her Weeze short for Louise, took me to Atlanta in the summers. Before moving to Florida, she had lived in Atlanta near Stone Mountain, in Decatur. We would take the railroad trip to Stone Mountain and I would climb to the top.

My grandfather was a woman chaser. So my grandmother would go to Atlanta and Ashville in the summers and take me. We were very close. She had no education at all, made it through the second grade. She played bridge and kept her mind sharp. She was quite bright, just not formally educated.

Weeze grew up in the area where they filmed "Gone With The Wind." We were up there when they did the very first premiere showing of the film in the Atlanta theatre. I remember it being like a museum, very ornate. All the stars from the movie were there because it was opening night. It was four hours long, so hard for me as a little kid to sit still through it. The people were yelling and cheering and carrying on. We had a memorable time.

When Weeze was 14-years-old, she came to Florida on the train. As the story goes, my grandfather saw her and immediately said, "You are going to live here with me now." And that was that. She did.

It was fascinating growing up, hearing stories of the Old South, and living in towns where the Old South was still very much alive. I didn't realize how unique my life would become, and how those experiences were very much a part of my future.

After seeing "Gone With The Wind," I spent all summer building whole castles and mansions and war scenes with weapons made of tools. Then the rains came, and washed it all away.

33

INFANTILE PARALYSIS

The two kids I played with in Atlanta for a month during summers, died of infantile paralysis and were kind enough to leave me with a dose of it. I became very ill at the end of one summer, so Weeze had to bring me back to Orlando. I got to Orlando and my mother had all the doctors in town come to see what they could do with me. One doctor said, "His appendix has to come out right now and he may have infantile paralysis."

My grandfather Dann did not believe in medicine. All twelve doctors in Orange County said I had to go to the hospital. My grandfather refused to allow me to go to the hospital to have the appendix removed. So all the doctors in town were on this little street on Greens Ave. by the golf course where we lived and all the people who worked at the golf course brought over guns so the doctors couldn't leave. My grandfather tried to find one to say I didn't have to be operated on. Finally the police came and convinced my grandfather that I'd have to go whether he liked it or not. It was almost too late. It had already ruptured. I was hospitalized and missed two-and-a-half months of school in second grade.

At the same time, I also developed infantile paralysis, which is why my arms and legs are shorter than they should be for my body. I should be six-feet-tall. If you look at photos of my father, that is how tall I should have been. At six and seven years of age, I ceased to grow because of the disease. I lived. It later made me want to be a doctor. It made me more stealth. I learned early on how to dodge bullets.

The Dann family home on Greens Ave. was built by Carl Dann, Sr. with the architect Sam Stoltz. When Sandy's grandmother Dann passed, she left the home to Sandy, where he still lives today.

CHAPTER 9, DANN AND LAND CONFLICTS

There was a huge ranch off Interstate Four towards Tampa from Orlando, before where Disney is now. You could buy all the land you wanted at that time for just $1 an acre, or just take it. It had value for growing citrus or ranching and that was about it. At the time, there was a single paved road to Windermere, which ended at a dirt road. It went on to the south into huge ranches. After two miles of dirt road, you pass one little house and fork off to the lake. The lake was six miles long at one time. The little house was the Dann Camp and the lake was called Lake Sandy. This is where grandfather Dann and the crackers all met for parties and fishing. It was a beautiful lake, crystal clear and forty–foot deep with deep springs which flowed into the big lake, Sand Lake. You could see the bottom in 40-feet of water. You could drink the water. It was that fresh. You could canoe from Lake Sandy to Sand Lake and go all around the edge and it would take a day and a half. They lowered the lake and drained it so the two lakes aren't connected anymore.

Sam Stoltz, the architect and builder, built the cabin with peckey cypress, with a two fireplaces, two sided with one chimney. It had a huge screened porch with a covered big roof. A covered dock with chairs seated 15 people, all open accessible by stairs. The ten-foot-tall dock had a diving board on top and underneath they would store canoes and boats.

As a kid, once we got old enough, we would drive out and use the camp. You could drive then at 13 or 14. During the war, no cars were made. My father was wise enough to get me a huge automobile that could drive through deep sand. It was a car that was used at Dubsdread. If you weren't a Cracker, and didn't know how to drive through sand, you weren't going to make it to the camp. Most people didn't understand that you take the air out of the tires to make them flatter so you don't sink from the weight of the car.

The surrounding area, all across the lake, was orange groves. All around the cabin was a bunch of trees, an oak stand. The caretakers lived across the lake.

All the land around the camp was owned by another family. There was a major conflict between the Dann family and the other family.

They wanted the land the camp was on and they tried to make my family leave. I was visiting Atlanta with my grandmother Dann and when I returned to Orlando the camp was burned. All the citrus trees on the camp property, of every type of fruit, was burned. The cabin and the dock survived.

Immediately after this, another fire broke out. Right after the annual citrus harvest was picked and stored in a big plant the size of several city blocks twelve miles from the camp, the plant burned to the ground with all the citrus in it. This ended the conflict between the Danns and that family, at least for that generation. My parents and the children of the other family were in school together, along with Bo Randall and others, where the feud continued.

My father sold the Dann camp to Disney around the early 1970's. It became Yogi Bear's Campsite. The construction workers building Disney World put their construction trailers there.

DANN CAMP FUN ADVENTURE

On a lighter note, as a young man in high school at the camp, I was cleaning up the place because I had some guys coming to spend the weekend. I was getting the docks and the canoes ready. I was naked working on the top of the roof over the water. It was hot as hell and I was sweating. A woman rode up on a horse from the other side of the lake. Well, she offered an interesting experience to a young man. After a long swim and a wonderful time, she got on her horse and galloped away.

She refused to give me her name or tell me where she lived. I followed her tracks around the lake to the other side of the other family's property. I saw where she was obviously the girlfriend of a guy who managed the property. When I got closer, the exterior was well protected by guards. I climbed up a tree. Half naked I was trying to explain myself to a guard who appeared, which was not accepted. I agreed to climb down. The guards said they were going to teach me a lesson. They told me to bend over on the dock. As the swung paddles at my behind, I was launched into the water naked for a long swim across the lake with a burning fanny. I happened to see the girl again when she was leaving in a train from Winter Park to go up north. She did recognize me, waved at me and gave me a wink. I never saw her again.

CHAPTER 10, GRANDFATHER WILLIAM CLAIBORNE LAWSON and GRANDMOTHER LAWSON

GENTLEMAN GRANDFATHER LAWSON INVENTED THE CABLE CAR

My mother's father was an attorney gentleman. My grandfather William Claiborne Lawson was the youngest person at that time to pass the Bar, at 19-years-old. He was brilliant.

Grandfather Lawson was an affluent, educated Virginia attorney who believed in education. He worked for the federal government at the patent office in Washington. He invented a system to get iron ore out of mountains using a cable car, an invention he gave to the government. He later invented a chair lift for snow skiing which was first used in Stow, Vermont. He patented 15 other inventions. He could memorize anything. He was a tinkerer and an inventor. He made fortunes on his inventions, then people would take the money from him. He was not a good money handler.

GRANDFATHER LAWSON STARTED THE TWO PARTY PO-LITICAL SYSTEM IN FLORIDA

At the time, there was only the Democratic Party, so he ran for office as a Republican, so there would be a two party system in Florida. He ran for Congress with his own money. He didn't win, but he did start the two party political system. People referred to him as "Senator."

He wrote a book entitled The Quest for Self-Government and I have one of the last copies.

I never saw him in anything other than a three-piece suit, even in the extreme heat of Florida. He lived to be 96. My grandmother lived to be 94. She was a survivor, too. Having passed 82 years now, I guess I got the longevity genes, too.

GRANDFATHER LAWSON DEVELOPED LAKE LAWSONA IN DOWNTOWN ORLANDO and GRANDMOTHER LAWSON MANAGED IT

Before they moved to Stone Island, my grandparents lived in Orlando in what is now Thornton Park. My grandfather didn't like Orlando because he thought there were too many people. I wonder what he would think now with three million people here?

Sandy remembers his grandparents on his mother's side, the Lawsons, always in formal attire as shown here with his aunt Elsie.

My grandmother Lawson owned 50 half-acres at Lake Lawsona, in the heart of downtown Orlando. My grandfather Lawson built magnificent houses in that neighborhood. If you head east on Central Blvd., the main downtown street, past the landmark Lake Eola, a few streets, you find Lake Lawsona.

She was a proper lady. She was always dressed to perfection like she was headed to church. She didn't drink or smoke. On Saturdays, she would pick me up from the house on Greens Ave. I'd go collect rent in that neighborhood. It cost 50 cents a week to live there at the time. The blacks lived on the land she owned that goes all the way to the cemetery. There were 50 homes on half-acre lots in heavy marsh. In the Orange County area there are over 1000 marshes and sinkholes. Our lakes come from sinkholes. When the sinkholes instantaneously sink hundreds of feet. Mayor Langford changed what is now a park there to his name.

So, the blacks usually didn't have their 50-cent rent money so they would give us what they grew in their gardens. So, we would ride around and collect the goodies, sometimes coins, and that is when she would tell me the stories of Old Orlando.

Grandfather and Grandmother Lawson, Aunt Elsie and mother Cathryn. The Lawsons developed Lake Lawsona in downtown Orlando then moved to a private estate on Stone Island in Sanford.

Proud four-year-old brother Sandy with his mother, Grandmother Lawson and sister Joanie.

Grandmother Lawson spent time with Sandy on Saturdays in Orlando. He would also visit their private island in Sanford on the St. John's River on weekends.

My grandparents bought 500-acre Stone Island on Lake Monroe across from downtown Sanford in Seminole County. They also bought 400-acres on the other side of Lake Monroe.

Stone Island is a five-minute drive to historic Enterprise, Florida, a quaint little town. The U.S. President spent his winters there as the Winter White House. Long before inland Orlando was developed, ferries would come down the St. John's River, bringing erudite New Englanders to grand hotels in Sanford. The island overlooks the Sanford skyline across Lake Monroe.

My grandparents built a causeway to get to their exotic island. Then they built a two-story, nine-bedroom, nine-bath house with a pool and a nine-hole golf course. They had two big grand pianos in the living room. They had a huge 30-foot high aviary with exotic birds of the world. My grandfather constructed his own ice maker. It was ten-foot high and a forty-by-forty-foot room. I would help to chip the ice to make blocks of ice to put in an icebox. This is before refrigeration as we know it today. He had a boat basin and docks. He spent 40-years building a boat and he died before he ever launched it. They had a black staff of 15 people. They entertained guests all the time.

I would stay with them in the summers in Stone Island, and my mother would take me there on weekends. From my grandfather, I would get an hour lecture on politics, both local and national. I would understand about a tenth of what he was talking about.

From the swampy cypress stands on Stone Island, you can see across Lake Monroe to downtown Sanford which was developed along the St. John's River before inland Orlando.

I liked visiting Sanford but I didn't have friends to play with. They would have me working and helping out when I was there. I would have time to explore some and found lots of Indian remains along the river bank. You can't get to that spot on the lake anymore because it's private property.

Sometimes there were Florida panthers on the island and the panthers would walk on the road because they have tender feet. Sometimes we would see them when we would have to bring a tractor to pull out the Cadillac when it got stuck on the dirt road. When I was a kid there was every kind of wild critter roaming free on Stone Island. You still see wild turkeys everywhere.

During the depression, they lost a lot of their money. My grandfather had a partner he trusted and he robbed him blind. He was too honest. So, now they had to be practical. The golf course became a cow pasture. The pool was set up to raise fish. The aviary became chicken coops.

After my grandparents passed, my uncle William sold the land and it was developed into a gated community with 130 estate homes. What was the three-hole golf course, is now a park. The original historic home was sold out of the family by his daughter. The home still stands and is owned by a family that winters in Florida.

Near the estate is Green Springs Park. It has only 28 parking spaces and walkways through native Florida land. You can climb up into the oak trees and dive into the crystal clear springs. Visiting there would give you an idea of the rural Stone Island I knew as a kid.

Sandy visited the historic home of his grandparents in 2015. The house was the original estate of the whole island. Now the island has been developed into an affluent gated community.

The Randall family who also were early settlers in Orlando. When my mother as a child moved to Stone Island there was no school so she came to Orlando for school.

My father and Bo Randall were the top people in the school. The Randalls are the famous knife makers. They make one-of-a-kind high end hunting knives. They also owned Champion Paper and Fiber and owned most of North Carolina, so he came from money and didn't have to work for money. The paper you write on, paper for books, everything paper they made money on. There were three Randall brothers who ran the paper company. Bo Randall and his wife Ruth were best buddies with my parents. They were the best looking and the best athletes and were in each other's weddings. The Randall house was on Dubsdread Circle by the club. During World War II, the Randalls built knives for the military. The military had never had a knife like that. It was made of a type of material that you can't break. The knives saved many lives during the war. Later in life they had two girls and one son.

For graduation from medical school, the Randalls gave me a Randall knife for a present. It has an ivory inlay of desert sheep and a bear on the handle. It's engraved with "Carl Dann, III." It's been a nice family relationship for generations.

Guess who had to take care of the two Randall girls growing up? Yes, me. In college they would visit and I'd have to drag them around on vacation to Chicago or New York. Patty Randall married one of my roommates at Chapel Hill. Doane Randall was married many times.

The Randalls owned property in the North Carolina mountains including the second tallest mountain in the U.S. I would visit them in summers over the years.

Sandy created one of the first speargun designs with the help of Bo Randall, an Orlando family freind and the maker of famous hunting instruments Randall Knives. He learned to fish in Orlando lakes where his family was among the very first settlers.

CHAPTER 13, MOTHER CATHERINE LAWSON AND SIBLINGS ELSIE AND WILLIAM

Cathryn Lawson was my mother. She was a blonde-haired blue-eyed attractive woman and when she walked in a room, every man turned. She was a petite five-foot-tall one-hundred-pound beauty. She was the youngest of three children. She was a decent golfer but not like my father. She was a great swimmer. She was born in Virginia, went to school in Orlando, then sent for a formal education in Switzerland.

She was feisty. She would have to be to be married to my father. My father was a great golfer, but a great gambler, too. The mafia came to Dubsdread every winter for six to eight weeks, and my father would gamble with them. One time my father kept losing and losing. He came home drunk and had to tell my mother, "These people have taken Dubsdread, the whole thing." The shoe shine boy came by and told my mother, "Miz Dann, 'dem men had someone standing behind Mr. Dann and was signaling his hand to the other players." My mother hopped on a train to Chicago, and went straight to mafia headquarters. She barged into the top penthouse of the Drake Hotel. Startled, they asked, "Cathryn what are you doing here?" She retorted, "I came to get my club back. You cheated my husband." Amused, the boss tore up the I.O.U. note and said, "You cheeky bitch, go on home." So, she went back with Dubsdread still in the Dann family.

My mother Catherine Lawson Dann presenting a trophy for a golf tournament at Dubsdread.

MOTHER CATHERINE "MAMA D" in BAHAMAS

Mama D was tough. I had a house in the Abacos where the family would get together for summer vacations. Behind the Bandit boat, I had designed a wooden bench pulled by a long ski rope. The kids could hang on to the bench to look for conch to dive for, or for fish to spear, or just to enjoy the coral reefs. They would signal when something was of interest, I'd stop the boat so they could dive. Well, Mama D was in her seventies by now and she wanted to get back there in the water with the kids. So she did. Her mask filled up with water to her eyes. She didn't complain. She never said a word. She was tough.

The boat the Dann family kept in their home in the Bahamas for family fun fishing, diving for conch, and exploring the Abacos. Mama D kept up with the younger family members.

The Danns house in Hope Town in the Bahamas before and after Hurricane Floyd.

AUNT ELSIE and UNCLE WILLIAM

Her sister Elsie Lawson married the composer Rudolph Friml. She was stunning and a beautiful actress and dancer. She was roommates with Helen Hayes in New York City and they did three plays together. She travelled to England and France and all over Europe. They were dining together at Tour d' Argent when Lindberg landed at the Paris Airfield LeBourget in 1927. My mother had many stories and adventures from travelling with her sister in Europe.

Her brother William was an attorney who quit law to become a land developer.

Stacks of photo albums were found in the Stone Island historic Lawson family home and now are stored in Sandy's home.
His aunt Elsie Lawson, as shown here, portrayed the gold-digger in "Dancing Mothers" at the Booth Theater in NYC. Her roommate, Helen Hayes, played the ritzy flapper.

CHAPTER 14, FATHER CARL DANN, JR.'s ADVICE ON GOLF VERSUS MEDICAL SCHOOL

My father was an only child born in 1909 in Orlando.

I always wanted to be a doctor as opposed to a golfer like my father. The top money winner might make $2,000 to $24,000. The only way pro golfers could make a living at that time was through gambling. They would come here to Orlando on the golf circuit back then which was only nine-months a year. In December to February, they came to Dubsdread because it was cold up north. They came to gamble. Most were nice to us, and good to me.

I asked my father if I could learn to play golf. He told me that after school, I would come to Dubsdread and practice with the golf pros. Then he would work with me. Then I would play 18 holes before dark everyday, and on weekends, I would play 36 holes a day.

I said, "Dad, when would I have time to hunt and fish and play with my buddies?"

He said, "You won't have time."

I said, "I don't want that."

He said, "Good," and he walked off.

My father was a world class amateur golfer. He was five time State Amateur Champion, a three time National Club Champion, Southern American Champion and runner-up twice. He was considered to be one of the best golfers in America.

Bok Tower sits on 4,000 acres at the highest point in the state. There is a golf course there surrounded by three beautiful lakes, a hotel and about 150 of the most enormous mansions. There are about 75 policemen on the property. There are no photos taken, no articles written about it, no apparent way in. It's very exclusive and private. These were the old money people who moved out of Palm Beach when the new money people moved to Palm Beach.

There was only one amateur tournament ever played there. The Walker Cup Amateur teams from America and Britain were invited to play.

My father had just married my mother and drove in to the tournament in a Model A Ford with a rumble seat, and was staying with the president of GM. Upon arriving, my father the jokester, with a servant greeting him asking him, "What would you like for breakfast, Sir?"

My father requested, "Caviar and fresh sardines if possible."

The servant responded, "Would 20 minutes on the patio be sufficient?"

There was a beautiful Cadillac convertible with ribbons tied all over it in the driveway. My father knew this was for first place and Bobby Jones, the greatest golfer of all time, was playing in the tournament against him. Bobby Jones won all four of the major amateur championships to become the greatest golfer that ever lived, then he went to law school and never became a pro. Well, my father wanted that Cadillac, so he won, but the Cadillac with all the ribbons was second prize. Everyone thought Bobby Jones would win, so the Cadillac was the second prize.

My father got this silver bowl, etched with the engraving, "Mountain Lake Club 1937, Invitational Tournament Championship, First Prize Won By Carl Dann, Jr."

My dad was a golfer and a gambler. This one he lost.

Sandy's dad was a golfer and a gambler according to Sandy.

Sandy's father Carl Dann, Jr. golfing with other famous golfers, Jimmy Johnson, Jay Byrd, Craig Wood, Byron Nelson and Sam Snead.

Sandy and Joanie by the Greens Ave. home Sam Stoltz fireplace when they were children and with new dogs as adults.

Nothing stops Joanie. She's a lot like both my mother and my father. You would never know her age. She's four years younger than me but acts 30 years younger. She's a great golfer. When she was growing up, she was on the golf course. I was busy digging tunnels and building tree houses with my friends. Remember I left for prep school in ninth grade and so she was in fifth grade and I was gone for 30 years while she perfected her sport.

She was the runner up of the Amateur State Championship in eleventh grade. She met a golfer guy on the east coast who won the Amateur State Championship. She married Dave Regan right after high school so no college. They had three kids. He was a big time golfer and won six pro tournaments. He lost his touch when he got anxious and started thinking too much about his shots. In golf, it has to be natural to win. He was gone all the time golfing so the marriage didn't stick.

Next she married a gambler, a dentist, and a third one, Steve. She's dating a great guy now.

Sandy's sister Joanie started golfing at a young age. She won the
State Amateur Championship and played with the women pros in
professional women's golf.

CHAPTER 16, EARLY EDUCATION AT ORLANDO'S PRINCETON GRAMMAR SCHOOL

Having a father who owned a golf course with a swimming pool, needless to say, my buddies at Princeton School thought I was fun. It was a charming time. The grammar school still exists in College Park in Orlando and has recently been renovated.

Orlando childhood friends Ted Eidson, Stu Gilman, Sandy Dann spearfishing in the crystal clear lakes and streams.
While sister Joanie was golfing, Sandy was hunting and fishing.

We walked on the all-dirt streets to school. We'd walk in deep sinking two to three-inches of sand and dirt, which would wear your feet off inside of shoes. So we walked barefoot to school until the fourth grade. In fourth grade, they made us wear shoes, and they paved the road.

One of my classmates was Bob Young, and his brother John Young was a year older than us. He was the first astronaut to walk on the moon. I didn't know him well. He was a loner who became one of the most famous people in the world.

Interesting enough, my first year of class, as a first grader, there were four seats at each table. One of the students became my amazing first wife and the mother of four of my children, Nancy Burcham. My wife died young of cancer. If ever there was an example of the good dying young, it was Nancy.

The other two students were Ara May Hishcock and Ray Lilly. We all stayed best friends throughout our lives. I graduated from Memorial, there were only two Junior High Schools at the time, Memorial and Cherokee, then I got sent away to prep school. My three friends that I started out with in first grade were number one, two, and three in their class in Junior High. I was in the middle.

They were all bigger than I was because of the infantile paralysis I had in second grade.

As a child, I was fascinated with medicine. I was always dissecting critters as part of my nature adventures. Two of my parents' closest friends were physicians, so on weekends, I'd work in hospitals and in operating rooms as the clean up boy. So, the die was cast for my desire to be a physician.

St. Marks 1952, on the dock with fish with Luther, Calvin, "Mac" (Walter McJordan,) Sandy Dann. Sandy and his childhood friends had many outdoor adventures in Orlando, Florida coastal areas and the islands, and continued to hunt and fish together throughout their lives. Several of his friends were sent to prep schools for education and they would return home for summers.

CHAPTER 17, WORLD WAR II, INFLUENCE OF IVY-LEAGUE MILITARY PILOTS

Everything changed when World War II started. I was in the fourth grade when the whole world changed, and Central Florida changed with it. What happened when the war was declared, Orlando became a military town. We had 12,000 people in the area. The military came and they moved 50,000 people here. It's difficult as I look back and now understand how severely our city was affected by war.

At that time, Florida had no medical school, or anything close to it during World War II. We were a little town. We had seven grammar schools, two junior highs and one high school.

Our country was not prepared for war. As I look back, those years completely changed the way we thought about the world. People came and went bringing new thought to our generation.

Dubsdread was turned into the officers club. The pilots trained, and marched and did exercises. It was a big education to learn about the world, from this little bitty town with dirt streets. At night in my room, I would sit in the open screened window listening to the educated pilots. I would listen to the all night going-away parties in the front yard. I would hear them saying their goodbyes, and slapping mosquitos, and the stories of what they had done in their lives. They would all propose to my mother. She was stunningly beautiful.

When they left the Air Force Base in Orlando, they would fly low over the club to say goodbye. Sometimes they would clip the tops of the big trees would and you would see the leaves all over the ground. I would wake up when they would leave. You would hear the engines through our open windows.

My mother was fascinated with the New England upper class, who were stationed here during the war. Their demeanor and activities were always gentlemanly. We were a cracker state and a cracker town at that time. These guys were Ivy League educated and the top Air Force pilots. There was a 62 percent mortality rate in their flight missions over Europe. They would fly the big B17s to England, then on to Europe on bombing runs. These were all Harvard, Princeton and Yale grads and they knew how to fly already from flying their own planes. The brilliant people were sacrificed first. The pilots were the best in the country and the navigators had to watch and keep perfect time in order to bomb their exact marks. They were the best of the best.

ROLEX WATCH

In the two-bedroom Dann home by Dubsdread, my grandmother added a room for the officers training here. There was not enough room in the barracks. Many people in Orlando were asked to add rooms to their homes for housing. And this is what I found, an antique Rolex watch.

This is one of the first Rolex watches ever made. The very first was made in 1905. I sent it to Rolex and they confirmed it was original and said there are no parts for it. In 1940 when it was made, it was worth $30. I had it appraised, it's priceless now. The most expensive Rolex to date is worth a bit more than $30.

I found it in 1991 in a high closet in the room where the officers stayed.

During the war, to feed the officers at Dubsdread, we had 50 acres where we raised crops. We also raised chickens and pigeons. I had to wring their necks sometimes. I didn't like that but they were good eating.

When the war was over, many people had fallen in love with Orlando from their time here. Some of the military people moved back here, rather than living with the cold New England winters. After the war, you would look around at all the new houses built all around the golf course. They wanted to retire and play golf and the town exploded after World War II. Martin Marietta moved its' military and space engineering here, which brought educated people. The boom started and hasn't stopped. It slows during the inevitable busts that always follow our booms, as in any economy.

CHAPTER 18, EDUCATION AT CHOATE PREP SCHOOL

My mother was determined to send me away to prep school with the New England aristocracy. My father and grandmother were against it. They didn't understand why I would need that type of education. As time passed, my mother got together with two of the family doctor buddies and my grandmother Louise, and a half dozen of the prep school people who had been stationed here, and they convinced my father that if I was going to be a physician, I would have to leave the state and go to prep school. She sent me to be trained like the wealthy New England pilots.

I'm in Orlando out hunting and fishing with my buddies and I didn't want to go to prep school to learn how to fly. I liked Orlando. I would leave Orlando that I loved for years to get my education, before I would return to live. I left in ninth grade and would not return until after my education at 30.

My mother took matters into her own hands. I finished ninth grade in Orlando. In 1947, I was off to Choate in Wallingford, Connecticut. It's twelve miles from Princeton.

My grandmother Lawson paid for me to go to prep school. I didn't realize at the time how much it cost her.

On my entrance exams, I passed English by one point, math and otherwise I had a 40 average score. I never did learn to write and spell well. I was a good reader. I was totally uneducated in other subjects. I was busy building tree houses and underground tunnels. I made A's and B's in Orlando, and failed my first year at Choate.

I left my little town and went to New England where they only wore coat and ties, like my mother's father. I wore t-shirts. I failed everything. These guys were in private schools all their lives, so I was very behind. These guys were all so far ahead of me. They had such a head start with private schools, and tutoring, and life expectancies of families who said, "This is what you do and how to do it."

In Orlando, I went to school and made ok grades. I had friends and I hunted and fished. At Choate, you were working or in school six days a week. Period. You had five hours off on Sundays. In study hall, you couldn't talk. If you weren't studying, you got a whack on the back with a stick. I had to figure out how to study. I took remedial classes, and passed the tenth grade the second year.

I caught up with the stiff competition. I went from failure to graduating Cum Laude, one of the top ten-percent in my class. It was competitive. These were not tacky people; fifty-percent had scholarships to Harvard, Princeton and Yale, including me.

NEW ENGLAND HOMES OF CLASSMATES

I never could come home. It took two days to get to school from Orlando. On breaks, I would visit classmates beautiful New England estates on acres of land. Their homes would be the size of a city-block. They would have 50 acres of immaculately manicured yards. I saw what real money was.

I would say, "Let's get your friends and have some fun." They wouldn't have friends, or maybe one friend, who was away at school. I had a bunch of friends that I would get together with if I was on break in Orlando. I didn't understand that type of life of the extremely wealthy families. I didn't' understand not having friends. They were controlled people. That's what it took to be privately trained and educated, hard work and discipline. They were totally spoiled with private education since birth. They didn't have the childhood adventures that I had with my friends. It was a different life.

CIRCUS FRIENDS IN NEW YORK CITY

On some five-day vacations, I would go to their exquisite homes in New York. We were in the city, walking down the main drag in Time Square. I saw this guy who was seven-feet-tall. I had never seen anybody that tall, so I was sort of looking at him. "What are you looking at boy?" he asked me. I told him I had never seen such a tall man. He asked what school I was attending. He could see from my suit and tie that I was in prep school. "I'm in the circus as the biggest guy in the country. Come with me," he said and led me into this alley to meet a midget two-and-a-half-feet-tall. These apartments were where the circus performers lived when they weren't working. He introduced me to another guy with two arms in his back and a guy with two eyes on the side of his head. "Tell us about this school, prep school boy," the largest man requested. I told them about me being different in my own way and trying so hard to catch up with those much more educated that I was. This was back when you mailed written letters by postal mail. I had to send them my grades and tell them how I was doing in prep school. They wanted to know every grade. They insisted I get better grades like I was their child. They sent me terrible chastising letters telling me I had to do my job as a student correctly. I was their pet prep school boy. I was amazed at how much they sent me for graduation. They were very generous. They sent me money for new outfits. I realized how important I was to them because I represented normalcy in a society they didn't understand at all. Follow me? I never knew what happened to them after that.

CLASSMATES AT CHOATE

The prep school study habits pay off. When I go back to reunions, 40 percent of my classmates are the heads of major companies.

Hendrick Smith was my suite mate in tenth grade at Choate. He later wrote the book The Russians, which becomes an important detail in one of my later adventures in Russia. He was the bureau chief of the New York Times in Russia for eight years.

One guy was the crew team coxswain. He's the guy who says, "Stroke, stroke, stroke," and sets the pace. Crew is a big sport in the Northeast. You get the littlest, skinniest guy, so you chose the guy who is 110-pounds and five-foot-two-inches. When I went back to a reunion, there was a big guy speaking on stage. It was him now six-foot-four-inches; he grew a foot after prep school. His family owned the Farmer's Almanac, which has 4 million copies in print in 48 translated languages. They hire the eight guys who are the best in the world at predicting weather. Mistakes? Yes, the worst was in 1884, there was a mistake in the printing office. They misinterpreted and reversed January for July, so it read, "It will snow in New England every day in July." Krakatoa in the Dutch West Indies blew up that year so it did snow in July! For two years, smoke covered the world from that volcanic eruption. The island was one-and-a-quarter miles high and the water under it was one-and-a-half-mile deep and it all blew up in one big puff. It killed tens of thousands of people and affected the world. That was an error in judgment for that guy's family, but it turned out fine. He was a neat guy.

GRADUATION FROM CHOATE
  Some of the wealthiest people in the country came to the graduation. We sat ten people to a table. My father sat next to Mrs. Roosevelt, the president's wife. My father told dirty jokes the whole time. It was so embarrassing.
CHAPTER 19, COLLEGE AND MED SCHOOL:

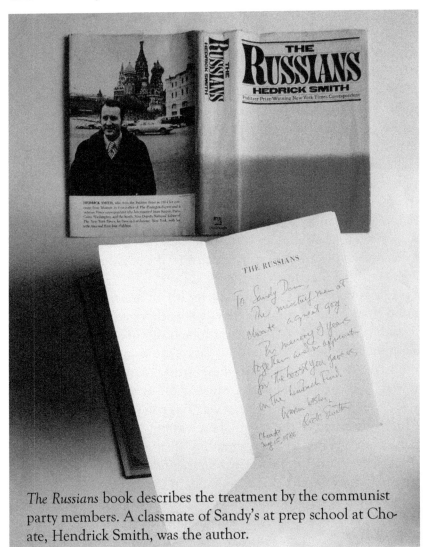

The *Russians* book describes the treatment by the communist party members. A classmate of Sandy's at prep school at Choate, Hendrick Smith, was the author.

CHAPEL HILL IS WHERE?
COLLEGE TESTING BY GOVERNMENT

After graduation from prep school came, everyone was being tested to go to war. In 1951, during the Korean War, you were either in school or in the service. Remember, at this time, we didn't have computers like we do today. Computers were big and bulky the size of an average house like this house and had little functionality. The government was testing all over the land for materials that would give them concepts of prediction. They were going around to schools to test for great perception. They would have a stack of papers with quiz questions of every subject, and give you three seconds to look at it and guess the answer to see how many you could get right. There would be ten paragraphs they would flash at you. If you answered correctly, they had to determine, did you guess, did you read that fast, or do you have something inert inside?

The military tested all of the prep school students. These two guys came back and called me into the president's office the next day to test me again and said, "You have survival instinct. You made the right decision in the three second glance more times than when you were given four minutes to answer the questions." I didn't know I was getting the answers right the first or the second test, but I answered all correctly on both tests.

It's complicated and hard to explain. It's an unusual part of the mind from ancient primitive times where they had to make instant decisions to survive. You glance at something and don't know you are understanding it. What seems unique to us now was automatic thousands of years ago to determine, "this is dangerous and this is not." Your primitive instinct which exists in some people tells you, "That leopard is facing that way, but will jump the other way." This instinct helped the government with my information, but also helped me as a hunter throughout my life to make instantaneous decisions for survival. I theorize that the infantile paralysis may have triggered this adjective primal memory in me.

They kept on with the tests and said, "We'd like you to sign up with the military service to do surveillance and you can go to Chapel Hill."

I said, "But I have a scholarship offered to Yale and Dartmouth and ..."

They said, "No, you will go to Chapel Hill."

I asked, "Where is it?"

I hated not going to Yale. Seven U.S. Presidents went to Yale. Twenty percent of my graduating class was going. I would have been with people who knew me personally instead of a place where I didn't know anyone, or even where it was.

Well, Chapel Hill is in North Carolina, actually on a hill in the middle of flatlands. In 1951, I got on a train to Raleigh with all my prep school clothes, and took the bus to Chapel Hill. I found out it was the communist center of the U.S. The Daily Worker newspaper was delivered to your doorstep every morning. When I got to my dormitory and met my two roommates, they immediately started talking about being communists and how they felt about our country.

Duke University is just ten miles from Chapel Hill and North Carolina State makes a triangle. It's the second biggest brain factory and it's in North Carolina. The whole area was filled with scientists in secret buildings; they were building a research center within the university system.

All the Secret Service guys gathered for a meeting at Duke at a fraternity house. They sent for me to come and asked, "So, how are you doing at Chapel Hill?"

My little smart ass decided to be quiet and polite, and just answer their questions.

I was a wrestler but they looked like professional wrestlers. They had perfect physiques and perfect hair; they looked military. They all looked alike. The Secret Service guys all take on a funky attitude. They don't flash a badge, but why else were they there? They never revealed themselves but one or two guys all lived in all the fraternity houses. I would see them around campus but they didn't go to classes.

I did as they said. I went around and listened to the professors in class talk about how they were totally against the U.S. I made notes that, "such and such is preaching this and a doctor is doing this." I made my notes, and put them in the mailbox as directed by the secret service guys.

I didn't realize at the time how the government was using my notes and they didn't want me to know. Sandy Dann is not that smart. Everybody else had to go into the service. It was war and the other students had to march in Navy uniforms. I just got to go about my business and study and have fun. I contributed in my own way.

I made friends. I had been captain of the wrestling team at Choate, so joined the wrestling team. A few of my fraternity brothers had also gone to prep school in New England and were wrestlers.

I was busy studying because I wanted to move on. I was stupid to take four years of school in three years. I missed a lot of playtime. I took classes dawn till dusk.

Interestingly, when I came back after summer vacation in New England, half the teachers and faculty at Chapel Hill were dismissed and 500 students were thrown out. The Daily Worker was no longer delivered to your doorstep each morning. I'm sure some of them were needlessly let go, but unfortunately, some people were clean and evidently, some were not.

After some 50 years have passed, I can say this. After my Chapel Hill days, they followed me and I continued to be a messenger. Not knowingly. I was a hunter and fisherman all over the world, in Mongolia, Russia, the Pacific and so forth. I would go on long trips out of the country and carry huge amounts of equipment because I'm a hunter. My wife will tell you, our suitcases never looked exactly the same upon return. The suitcases were being changed out, inside the compartments I would be transporting things.

I never paid attention raising kids and living my life. When I got away to hunt, I didn't pay attention to what was in my suitcase. People would ask, my own wife would ask, "How did you get back from Russia when a war broke out? Who was helping you?" Unbeknownst to me, people in Russia working for the U.S. government got me and my hunting buddies out without saying anything. The U.S. embassy closed down and people could not tell you they were working for the government. How I survived? I just didn't know I was in that much trouble. Trouble would find me all over the world, in remote places, as I continued to hunt and fish and explore. And the government and their packages would find their way home to the U.S. again, with me.

FRATERNITY PLEDGE AT CHAPEL HILL
I joined Phi Delta Theta fraternity. As a young pledge, a brother told me to get my car. We went to the gas station and filled up the tank. He told me to drive. We went through Pinehurst, then through South Carolina, we ended up in Daytona Beach 500 miles away. He wanted to stay but I had to get back to class. We went out on the beach.

He said, "I always wanted to come here."

Then we got back in the car and I drove all night to get back to go to class. We did a lot of fun things. Jack Kerouc would have felt at home with us.

FRATERNITY BOOK CLUB
In the fraternity, I was friends with a chap who graduated from the University of Miami and was in dental school. He convinced me to join the book club that met every Tuesday at 5 p.m. with five guys who were all from Florida. We made perfect martinis out of sophisticated equipment I had borrowed from the science lab. You got one martini, chatted, then went to dinner. You always wore coats and ties in the fraternity house.

We got bored with our own stories, and we started inviting guests in once a week. We invited friends, and teachers. A year later, the dean of the University of North Carolina summoned me. Needless to say, I was nervous walking into his office, which was half the size of a ball field.

His secretary told me when I asked her why I was summoned, "I think you have a problem. You're in big trouble."

After waiting ten minutes to get to His Majesty's desk, he also affirmed what his secretary said, "Mr. Dann, you are in big trouble."

Shaking, I asked, "What kind of trouble?"

He said, "I have not been invited to your book club."

So, we resolved that. We keep the book club framework alive here in Orlando. We meet at the University Club; not the same fraternity brothers, but the same idea.

GIRLS IN COLLEGE

Girls were not involved. Chapel Hill was a male school at the time. At the big dances, not to worry, the girls all showed up in their fancy dresses.

Some were in the dental school to be dental hygienists. They didn't let girls in to Chapel Hill till their third year of college to make sure they were serious about studying and not just at college looking for husbands.

There was one beautiful and smart girl there who came from Miami. She was six-foot-one and an unbelievable athlete. We studied together in the library six days a week. She was in a sorority and would pick me up to go to the frat houses and drink till we collapsed. She went on to be a big doctor at the University of Miami.

We took ten or eleven of Florida's best looking women to Chapel Hill with us. One was Miss Florida. We took them from FSU and University of Florida. My wife to be came up, too, she was one of them. We grew up with all of them. Who knew they would all look like that in college? Nancy and I were buddies all the way through school, she came to Chapel Hill, we dated, and we married.

At Chapel Hill, I was the big man on campus because I brought all the pretty girls from Orlando!

SUMMERS DURING CHAPEL HILL

One great summer in college, I got home from Chapel Hill. A guy from a wealthy family, going to Rollins College, had a new woody station wagon. Stu Gilman, me, and this guy traveled in the new car up north to see these two girls they had met at Rollins. The girls had been thrown out of Rollins because they fornicated with two entire fraternities. They were wild girls. So we drove to see them at the top of the lakes in New England. It was a beautiful place. If you look at a map of the Great Lakes, it's the furthest over by Chicago on the way up to the Canadian border. The island stuck out like a peninsula in the lake. I didn't know where I was going but it didn't matter; it was a delightful summer. The girls treated us like kings. The guy married one of the girls later but the marriage didn't last long.

I got a job building war material. I worked in a big plant building a boat 200-feet long. The boat was to run next to carriers to protect them and carry crews of 100 people. Our job was to bolt the boat together. We would bet on how fast we could do it. We got a raise every week. I was working about as far away from Orlando as you could get and still be in the States. It was fun. I came back with a concept of what hard work is all about. It helped me in school to understand what full-tilt work is all about. I never had to work like that before. I applied the concept to my studies at Chapel Hill, and finished four years of studies in three.

DENTAL SCHOOL IDEA
  One classmate from Miami was in dental school. His name was Tom Lasalle.
  He said, "You don't want to go to medical school. All you talk about is hunting and fishing all of your life. You can't be a physician and go sailing in Tonga, hunting in Africa, exploring in Mongolia, and all the other things you want to do. Now, you can be a dentist and see your patients and take time off if you schedule it right. Better still, you can be an orthodontist, a good one, and you can see all your patients in one month or six weeks. Carry extra staff and you can be gone for a month. To resolve your travel bug and desire to see and enjoy the whole world, with a salary that will allow you to do it, this is what you need to do."
  So, I took his advice and that is what I did.
  Chapel Hill is the oldest University in the U.S., not a college, but a university.
  We built the best dental school in the U.S. at that time. Chapel Hill started the dental school at that time and recruited the best talent in the world to teach and do medical research. They opened their doors and immediately became the number one dental school in the world. Many of the students became teachers and one started a dental school in Florida and another in Texas. You studied because you were either making your grades or in the military service. We students wanted to be in college and not in the military, so we studied.
  My friend Ben Barker told the dean at that time, "I want to be dean of this dental school."

The dean said, "Graduate number one in your class. Get a degree in business management. Work for a huge corporation. Then come back and we'll make a deal."

He came back many years later and asked the dean, "Would the head of Kellogg, one of the largest corporations in the world, be sufficient for me now to be dean?"

He became dean and I've visited him over the years. It's a wonderful school. We've stayed friends and travelled together to some great places.

CHAPTER 20, DR. DANN, THE ORTHODONTIST PROFESSIONAL / GATOR ORTHODONTIC GROUP

I started a study group here in Florida, which allowed me to go to all of these exotic places and to also feed seven, eight, nine kids, a bunch of little Indians. I could work like crazy and then be gone. I was still working on what Sandy wanted to do. If I was going to go into dangerous remote hunting venues, chances are eventually it would catch up with me. My patients nor my family would never suffer.

So, my idea, how it came to me was, "I'm not a rich little fart so how can I afford to do what I want to do and not risk handicapping my family?"

How to maintain my lifestyle was to start a study club with the very best orthodontists in Florida, which we called the Gator Orthodontic Study Club.

We assembled the best orthodontists in the state. We had the best of the best. Five became Presidents of the Florida Dental Society, four were Presidents of the Southern Dental Society and one was the President of the National Dental Society. We started with nine guys who were interested. We met two or three times a year at each other's offices. We'd also go someplace fun like the Bahamas, Scotland, France and other interesting places.

The plan was to first change all of our wills. Gator Orthodontic Group owned our practices. The group would take over your practice if you died. They would take care of running it until it sold. We knew how to run it and we knew what it was worth. We'd keep the wives and children out of it.

Also, I had people to cover when I was gone. If I was going to Mongolia, I never knew for sure when I would get back, or if I would ever get back. To be comfortable, every two years, the entire group would spend two days at your office learning how you work and where everything was. You had to keep the families out because they have no clue about the business and it would go down the tube. Within six weeks, practices would be gone. Maybe 500 patients are coming to you, but something happens to you, they leave and they aren't coming back. So, with the Gator Orthodontic Group, our investment would be protected until sold. It was greaseless. The very next day, someone would step in and take care of the business. The women were happy. The families were happy. It worked like a charm. We had a hundred people begging to get in. Several people copied our system. It worked perfectly.

Sandy with world record marlin, 247 pound on 12 pound test line in Panama in 1967. Sandy's fishing trophies were often recorded in stacks of Orlando newspaper *Sentinel Star* articles, and also in national fishing magazines and periodicals.

With his flexible career, Sandy Dann could hunt and fish. He held world records for marlin fishing. Sandy orchestrated his career so he could travel and hunt. He is a great example to follow your passions. Read about his worldwide adventures in his book *Dreadful Errors in Judgment.*

In the 1960's his second wife Barbara was one of the top female fisherman in the world. She caught the biggest marlin that any woman or any man had ever caught at that time. She held the record for 20 years. They were invited all over to fish in the Caribbean and Pacific.

The dining room in Sandy's historic Dann Greens Ave. home hosts some of his trophy fish added to the decor during his era.

Sandy's career gave him the freedom to follow his passion for ourdoor adventure with family and friends. He and Shelia honeymooned in Zambia on a safari in 1980.

Above and right friends hunt birds in Uruguay at his El Saladero Ranch.

CHAPTER 21, DOUBLE EAGLE RANCH
ON ST. JOHN'S RIVER

As a young professional, I was working but liked to get into the outdoors as much as possible. In 1960, over 50 years now, a wealthy friend said, "What we need is a ranch. I've been fiddling around with this plot of land that goes 40 miles in either direction on the other side of the St. John's River. I've heard they might sell it." Two families, over five generations, owned 12-miles of riverfront property on the St. John's. We heard they didn't intend to develop it. We got in a Piper Cub with a pilot and flew over and there was nothing but nature for 50 miles to A1A along the coast.

There were a few little, bity towns with four or five houses on the river. The whole country was settled along the rivers for transportation. The historic town of Geneva near the camp, still has churches from 1875. It still has orange groves, cows and horses in an old-world community. There's a half-mile wide lake there that was a sink hole, only knee-deep. The birds love it. It's filled with bald eagles. If you dig around the riverbanks, you can find little goodies of history. We've dug up artifacts of gear and parts of guns from the Civil War where soldiers camped and cooked. One of Abraham Lincoln's killers lived along the banks; it was before Orlando existed.

There was the Fort Lane Park on the St. John's which was the old Indian Trail. The kids and I found so many historical objects there. The State shut it down.

The St. John's River runs north. There are only two in the world that do so. The other one is in Africa, the Amazon, and I spent a month there hunting. The animals are all over this marshland. There are deer, turkey, and cows running around all over.

The aerial photos showed some timber. We bought this two-and-a-half by one-mile, 1040-acre swamp. The highest land is only three-feet above sea level. It was filled with 500-year-old cypress 5-feet in diameter. Cypress is bug resistant and bugs can't eat it like other woods, so it's ideal for buildings made to last.

My parents said there is only one investment worthwhile and that is property. For example, if you buy a ranch at $400 per acre, and

Sandy at the entrance to Double Eagle Ranch in 2014. He has owned the ranch since 1960. His parents advised him to invest in raw land. Both of his grandfathers made fortunes in real estate development in early Florida. Sandy replaced the sign at the entrance in early 2015.

now it's worth $4500 per acre, the question is what can you buy with the profits?

The government's depreciation of the dollar can destroy your profits. A profit is really what is the money worth, what can it buy.

A massive fire burned the property at Double Eagle Ranch, leaving behind this graveyard of cypress tree trunks. Some of the land has been re-seeded with new trees.

So, you have to time your investments and sales. While the dollar goes down in value, land is more likely to increase in value. My father asked me, "What do you charge for a two-year case?" I answered, "$345." He asked, "When you quit practicing orthodontics, what can you charge?" I answered, "Obviously nothing." He asked, "What did you pay for your first new car, that big Caddy?" I answered, "$1500." And he asked, "What's it worth today?" I answered, "Nothing." He summarized, "Land will always keep up with the economy and the value of a dollar."

My friend said, "You put up fifty-percent and I'll put up 50-percent. I'll put you in charge and expect you to make a profit and run it."

I didn't have the money, so he agreed to put up the purchase money and negotiated the deal. Now it was my job to figure out how to get into the land to the ponds we saw in the photos.

Sandy had two ponds dug at the ranch. Irrigation from a well refills the pond when it's not rainy. The fountain is both aesthetic and functional to circulate the water so it doesn't breed mosquitos.

The land is on the east side of the St. John's River out of Sanford. On State Road 46, you cross the river on a bridge at the Volusia County line leaving Orange County. The Jolly Gator Fish Camp is on the left. When I was a kid, you had to take a ferry across. Now you are in the marshlands and there's a little dirt road which goes two-miles along the river where the old Crackers lived. The homes were built on Indian mounds made by Native Americans as they piled up all the garbage where they camped and ate. Over thousands of years, the trees grew along the water front. That is how you can tell there is higher land, by the trees.

It was primitive land. So, from this little dirt road, I had to cut a road two-and-a-half miles into our property to get a car in. The Crackers in the area had equipment to help me. I hired them to bring their trucks and dig ditches and use the dirt to make the road between the two ditches. After we put in the road, we put fences all

A caretaker drops corn from this drum so deer come to eat. He also feeds the fish in the stocked pond. Fishing is usually good except the year a giant alligator moved in and ate all the fish.

the way around the property. You need fences so cattle don't just wander off and disappear. While building the fences, I climbed up into this huge oak tree to get the lay of the land inside the property. I had a good idea after flying over it several times. Surrounded by the swamps were oak trees encircled by cypress trees, so I knew there was dry land inside. I waded in there and it was a good place to build a Cracker cabin.

We needed to earn some income before we could build the cabin. We built a shack on the edge of the property and added cattle and hired a guy to watch the cattle. We would timber the land to make money but had to make dirt mounds to plant the trees, you couldn't just plant them in the swamp.

I finally found and old Cracker, who was 74-years-old and a retired builder, who could help. I brought him out and we waded out to

The porches are furnished for entertaining. Panoramic views include both eagle nests, the two ponds, the cypress trees, and lots of Florida animal life.

the site. I dusted a place in the ground and in the sand, I drew a picture of what I envisioned. I wanted 16-foot screened porches on three sides. I wanted a sleeping porch with six beds. Inside I wanted an open living room with kitchen and large fireplace and two bedrooms and bathrooms inside. He watched and said, "Yep." I said, I'll get someone to draw plans. He responded, "You done drawed 'em."

I told him I would give him money for materials and he could get started. He said he had been curing cypress for 25-years and it was ready to use for a cabin such as this one that would last for one hundred years, so he didn't need money. He used his own tools and materials over a two-year period. He had a kid that helped him who brought him food to the camp site while he built the cabin. I got the call, "Dr. Dann, come look at the cabin." I said, "It's beautiful. It's perfect. I wouldn't change one thing. How much do I owe

Sandy in 2014 in the living room of Double Eagle Ranch. The cozy space is warmed by original art and arifacts. The turkey feathers number the wild turkeys Sandy shot at the ranch.

you?" He said, "Nothing. You done paid me." He died two weeks later. Building the hunting camp cabin gave him something to do. It broke my heart when he died. His name was Mr. Johnston.

Now us men had a hunting camp to hunt and be men. It was a great place to hunt and fish and entertain and, mostly, just be quiet. We also had a lot of parties out here. We'd have ten guys out here for the weekend raising cane. We could shoot guns and not bother people. In either direction, the closest person was 15, 20 or 30-miles away. We would build bonfires and enjoy our friendships sitting up all night around the fire in our getaway place and slap mosquitos and tell stories. The most fun thing is that people could talk about things that you couldn't talk about in civilization. You could tell dreams that you have and talk about the way that things should be.

We kept a ranch wagon to haul everyone around and we'd hunt all kinds of animals during the day. I had so much fun with all the kids here. Lawson is the only hunter.

We added roads to get all around the property to explore and hunt. We filled the cabin with Florida paintings and animal horns from our hunts. I put a feather for each wild turkey I shot here on the fireplace. I shot 51. There is a stream running through the camp and we dug two ponds. We added sheds for the horse stables. We added feeders for the stocked fish-ponds and corn feeders for deer. We dug a 150-foot well for fresh water. We added a fountain to keep the water moving and could pump water from the well to keep the ponds full.

The ponds were full of other things, too, reptiles. One year I said, "We don't have any fish. All the fish are dying." No, our stocked pond of fish were being eaten by a giant 14-foot alligator in the pond. They move along the ditches on the sides of the roads and they wander around the property. He wandered off and the fish were replenished.

One eagle roost was on one side and another on the other. The babies would come back the next year. That is how we named it Double Eagle.

My partner got divorced and married a girl that was difficult. He died a few years later and left her with the property. She was totally impossible. She and her buddies and other men were carrying on around the camp. I didn't come up to the camp much for ten years because of her. She got married to some guy in Canada and I got people then to buy her share of the property. My wife Shelia bought a third and friends bought 150 to 200 acre parcels. We still own the house on Dragonfly Run.

The family that owned the land around the camp sold it and made three gated communities in a 24-by-35-mile area. There are now 175 houses with 10 to 15-acre lots on the river. The rest will stay a park. It's unique because the State doesn't have jurisdiction over the land. The community has it's own police department, and fire department. The people who live around the camp want to be away from car horns and planes. It's a different type of life, not city life. The people here have toys to enjoy the land. By their riverside

Double Eagle Ranch is in the middle of
nowhere. There is no noise. There is nobody
around. It's so quiet. People go out there
and ask, "What's wrong with this place?"
I answer, "Nothing. It's perfect."

homes, they have small planes in the front yards, pontoon boats, canoes, rowboats, anything that floats.

There were three fires. One was really tragic. The government put in power lines on the edge of the property. One of the transformers blew up and started a fire. The government never gave us a dime for the massive destruction. The fire was so severe that it burned down all the trees. Over 300 firemen volunteered from all over the country to drop aerial water bombs. The firefighters battled in 130-degree heat for 20 hours. They loved doing it. Can you imagine trying to breathe? That one burned the whole ranch down including those majestic cypress trees. We are still recovering from that one. Just the way life is. We replanted pine trees which will take 25-years till harvest and we lease the land to a rancher with 100 head of cattle.

It's in the middle of nowhere. There is no noise. There is nobody around. It's so quiet. People go out there and ask, "What's wrong with this place?" I answer, "Nothing. It's perfect."

Sandy in 2012 hunting with Laddie. The Danns added two Jack Russell puppies to thier long line of canines. They named the pair Bonnie and Clyde after the hunting dogs from their El Saladero Estancia in Uruguay.

CHAPTER 22, ORLANDO IS HOME

Where I live in Orlando is home. I left here for 30 years getting educated, but returned to the place that I love. I have a lot of friends here. It's comfortable here. I'm sorry I lost the place in the Bahamas to the 40-foot surge of Hurricane Floyd. My son-in-law and daughter own it now. I miss the estancia in Uruguay. We were offered four times more than we paid for it, so the partners said it was time to cash it in. We sold the camp at Sand Lake. Disney came in and bought up all the land in that area a few years later. We would have gotten more. We still have Double Eagle Ranch for a retreat.

My family sometimes tells me I lecture them. I'm sharing my knowledge. They will understand that one day. As much as you love Orlando, you can't just sit here in your comfy life and not know what the rest of the world is about. So I sent them to prep school. That is not the same as going to other countries and staying for a month at a time. It's not the same as seeing first hand what other countries think about America and why.

So my family, especially my grandfathers, impacted me greatly. For my own future generations, I would like for them to remember that I tried to give them a good education. I would have them understand the planet, and how to survive. I would want them to remember that I took them on trips to show them the world. I took care of family and friends. I did things in life that were enjoyable and fun and I laughed a lot. My grandparents passed on to me that the most important thing is to find humor in life.

Sandy, Shelia and "all the little indians" as he affectionately refers to the children and grandchildren. The hub of the Dann family is the Greens Ave. home that Sandy inherited from his grandmother Dann.

Sandy and Shelia in their living room in the historic Sam Stoltz designed home built by Sandy's grandfather Dann.

RELATED BOOKS ON SANDY DANN both published in 2012

The Hunt For Nirvana
The Gentlemen Ranchers of El Saladero, Uruguay
A Collection of Stories and Images from 2004 to 2011

THE GIST: El Saladero created an impressive investment opportunity and intense bonding for the avid hunters, the novice hunters they coached, and the awestruck guests who marveled at the once-in-a-lifetime tips to the Uruguay estancia. In the book, meet the investors of the ranch as they fondly recall their experiences there with friends, loved ones, and each other.
The book was commissioned from El Saladero investors as a surprise thank you gift to Sandy and Shelia Dann who were key members of the ranch.

Dreadful Errors in Judgment
The Wild Worldwide Stories of Native Florida Outdoorsman
Carl "Sandy" Dann, III

THE GIST: I have a long list of dreadful errors in judgment. How I lived through them, nobody knows. It just wasn't my time. I have been bitten by everything including fish, barracudas, snakes, black widow spiders, and this and that. I grew up in Orlando and have hunted and fished all over the world. I hunted in Mongolia, Pakistan, Canada, North America, South America, and over 15 times in Africa. I went to the Nile basin where the natives had never seen a white person and they wanted to kill us. I've been sailing all over the world. The fear left me somewhere along the line. I've done a lot of stupid things. I had a lot of close calls. There were a hundred times when I should have died. But the stories are usually funny. And I'm still here to tell the stories and laugh with my friends about all of our dreadful errors in judgment.

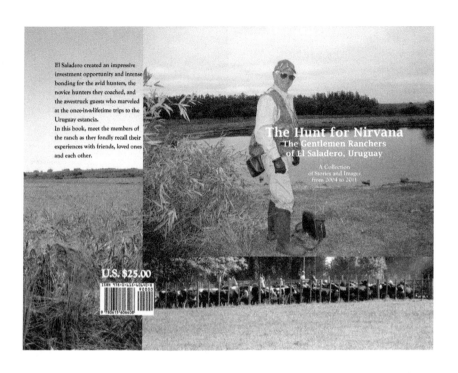

El Saladero created an impressive investment opportunity and intense bonding for the avid hunters, the novice hunters they coached, and the awestruck guests who marveled at the once-in-a-lifetime trips to the Uruguay estancia.

In this book, meet the members of the ranch as they fondly recall their experiences with friends, loved ones and each other.

The Hunt for Nirvana
The Gentlemen Ranchers of El Saladero, Uruguay

A Collection
of Stories and Images
from 2004 to 2011

U.S. $25.00

ISBN 978-0-615-60440-8

Dreadful Errors In Judgment

The Wild Worldwide Stories of Native Florida Outdoorsman Carl "Sandy" Dann, III

Carl "Sandy" Dann, III shares his adventurous Hemmingway-esque tales of hunting, fishing, sailing and exploring all over the world. His lighthearted delivery makes the most horrific circumstances humorous, as he recounts how he survived in each precarious dangerous situation. The book triggers wanderlust in the reader. Sandy's story also inspires creative thinking to strategize family and career to enjoy a life of living out a dream. *Dreadful Errors in Judgment* is a must read for outdoor enthusiasts and anyone interested in Florida history.

U.S. $28.00

ISBN 978-0-615-75560-5

Black Marlin Record On 12-Pound Line

Near Death Adventures
Big Game Hunting,
World-Class Marlin Fishing,
Spearfishing, Sailing, Diving

I did things in life
that were enjoyable
and fun and
I laughed a lot.
My grandparents
passed on to me that
the most important
thing is to find
humor in life.

In Jan. 1015, East Lake
Historical Society arranged for
a private tour of the Sam Stoltz
designed homes in Sorrento,
including the cabin built and
owned by Sandy's grandfather
Carl Dann, Sr. He is photo-
graphed here in one of the
historic homes ... enjoying life,
having fun, and laughing.

find
humor
in life

CPSIA information can be obtained at www.ICGtesting.com
Printed in the USA
LVOW05*2351170315

430859LV00001B/1/P